Louisa E. Litzsinger

Violets Under the Snow

A collection of short poems

Louisa E. Litzsinger

Violets Under the Snow
A collection of short poems

ISBN/EAN: 9783337254216

Printed in Europe, USA, Canada, Australia, Japan

Cover: Foto ©Thomas Meinert / pixelio.de

More available books at **www.hansebooks.com**

VIOLETS
: : : : : UNDER THE SNOW

A

Collection of Short Poems

BY

LOUISA E. LITZSINGER

The Blind Poetess of St. Louis County, Missouri

CLAYTON, MO.
THE PEOPLE'S ADVOCATE PRESS
1898

A

Collection of Short Poems

BY

LOUISA E. LITZSINGER

The Blind Poetess of St. Louis County, Missouri

CLAYTON, MO.
THE PEOPLE'S ADVOCATE PRESS
1898

This booklet of sacred verse has been published by the author at the request of friends. A number of the little poems have been contributed, from time to time, to the St. Louis County papers, and through them have won for the author the title of "Blind Poetess of St. Louis Co."

Yours truly,

    Louisa E. Litzsinger.

VIOLETS. UNDER. THE. SNOW.

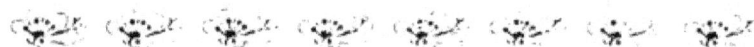

Violets Under the Snow.

YOU have heard of the little violets
    That blossom under the snow;
You have heard how they lift their sweet, blue heads,
    When the gentle breezes blow:
When the bright, warm sun, with its friendly rays,
    Has removed the snow and ice —
How they scent the air with their sweet perfume,
    Making Earth a paradise.

But they wait for the sun to melt the snow
    With its warm and beaming rays;
Until then, they will hide their little heads
    And their beauty from our gaze.
And so, in the depth of the human heart,
    There are graces rare and sweet,
Of a brighter hue and a sweeter scent
    Than the blossoms at our feet.

But they sleep till the Sun of Righteousness
    Shall pierce to the depths within
And remove the crust that enshrouds the heart
    In its unbelief and sin.

Yes, they lie, as dead, in their cold retreat,
 And their fragrance will be lost,
Till the holy Sun, with its warmth and light,
 Shall remove the Tempter's frost.

Let us hasten, then, with the Gospel Sun,
 To the regions dark and cold,
That its warmth may remove its frost of death,
 And the seeds of Life unfold.

Oh, that every heart could but feel the warmth
 Of redeeming Love and Grace!
How the golden fruits of a Saviour's love,
 Would the fruits of sin displace;
How the Earth would teem with the violets sweet
 Of a holy faith and love—
Like an Eden fair, as it was of old—
 Like the Paradise above.

A Bow in Bereavement's Cloud.

Art thou lonely, dear bereaved one,
 Does the world seem dark and drear?
Is there naught that offers comfort,
 Naught that offers light and cheer?
Doth it seem that all hath vanished—
 All thy treasure, all thy light,
With the dear departed loved one—
 Draping all the world in night?
Doth it seem that he hath taken
 With him to that world of bliss,

All the sunshine and the gladness,
   Leaving naught but gloom in this?
Is thy noonday void of sunshine,
   Are the roses at thy feet
Void of fragrance, once so cheery,
   Once so comforting and sweet?
Is the rare, harmonious music,
   Naught but discord to thine ear—
Void of all its soothing pow'rs,
   Once so full of hope and cheer?
Are the words of human friendship
   Hollow, unavailing, vain—
Loving sympathy but empty—
   All one dismal, mournful strain?
Yes, ah, yes! for earthly splendors,
   Earthly treasures rich and rare,
Bring no comfort, peace or balsam
   To the Soul in dark despair.
E'en the source of human friendship—
   Human sympathy and love—
Be it e'er so deep and tender,
   Adequate it cannot prove.

But there is a source of comfort,
   Yea, the only Source, indeed,
All-sufficient, all-sustaining,
   In our darkest hour of need.

Lift thy tearful eyes to Heaven!
   See the bow of promise there:
"Blest are they that mourn"; ah, sad one,
   How it beams with radiance fair.

"I'll not leave thee nor forsake thee:
　I am with thee, child, and lo!
All Earth's waters of affliction,
　They shall not thine heart o'erflow."
'Tis the darkness that surrounds thee,
　Stimulates thy grief and fears,
Morning light will bring thee gladness,—
　Joys for sorrows, smiles for tears.
When the darkness all has vanished,
　"When the mists have cleared away,"
When life's crosses thou beholdest
　In the light of perfect day,
All thy griefs will shine as blessings,
　Thy bereavements all will prove
Benedictions from the Father,
　Chast'nings from the hand of Love.

Solitude.

They wonder why I stole away from out the noisy throng,
Where merry voices ring aloud, in laughter jest and song,
Where all are happy, bright and gay, without a single care:—
They wonder why I would not stay to join their pleasures there.
But sought a poor companion in that dry and tedious book,
Or chose to sit and meditate in some dark, quiet nook:
And so they come with tender words to call and pity me:
They think I'm sad and lonely here, but, ah! they cannot see
How many cheering friends are nigh, though seemingly alone.
Nor can they see the light which all around me here is thrown.
Alone! ah, no, I'm not alone; here all is bright and fair:
For hosts of white-winged Angels, seem to hover round my
　　　chair.
Congenial friends, though far away, seem present with me here,

Though absent in the body, still I feel their spirits near.
They bless me with their kindly smiles and with their voices
    sweet,
They sing to me in Heav'nly strains, to make my joy complete.
'Tis here sweet memory proves my friend, and takes me back
    once more.
Away from care, to live again in happy days of yore,
And here the Angel of sweet hope, doth hover kindly near,
Doth whisper tenderly that I have naught of ill to fear,—
That He will still attend my steps where'er my path may lead,
That He will ne'er forsake me, but will prove my friend indeed.
He bears me on His airy wings to scenes of light and love—
He gives a foretaste of the store of better things above.

So here I taste my sweetest joys: here all my troubles cease.
And here my Soul enjoys the calm of sweet and tranquil peace.
But this they cannot understand who love the busy throng,
Who love to join the revelry of boist'rous shout and song;
But just within that noisy crowd, where solitude's unknown,
'Tis there I'm lonely and distrest, 'tis there I'm quite alone.

Resignation.

When hard afflictions press me, and disappointments come,
When shadows of bereavements have crossed my happy home,
When sweetest joys I've cherished and dearest hopes depart,
When brightest plans are thwarted which long have stirred my
    heart—
Whate'er my heavy trials, my heart is not dismayed,
Since I've a loving Father in whom my trust is stay'd :
He knows my bitter anguish, He counts my falling tears,
Knows all my pains and heart-aches, my griefs and direst fears:
He knows my hopes and prospects, my wishes ev'ry one,
And aught his love denies me, I know is kindly done:
He cares for me and loves me, and were it best, I know
He would deny me nothing— would lavishly bestow:

And when he has deprived me of ought I'd fain possess,
I know his love consid'reth my highest happiness.
For would a loving Father, so gentle, good and mild,
Have sent these hard afflictions on his beloved child,
Were it not on a mission of tender love and care?
So, as 'tis hard to sing now, I'll seek relief in prayer.
I mourn my pride and weakness, lament my stubborn will,
Whene'er my voice refuses to sing his praises still;
I know he is my Father, my best and truest Friend,
He marks my whole life's journey, and paves it to the end:
He loveth whom he scourgeth, and chast'neth every one
Whom his great heart receiveth, and all is kindly done.
Then why should I not love Him, and trust my Father still—
Strive both in bain and blessing to do his holy will!
Our griefs and disappointments of which our hearts lament,
Are ministering Angels on kindly missions sent:
And when their work's accomplished, our darkness turns to day:
For lo! we're one step higher upon the Heav'nward way.
When Earthly hopes deceive us, and Earthly joys are fled,
We set our heart's affections on Heavenly things instead;
Bereavement's tear must purge us and purify our love--
Must strengthen ties of friendship, and selfish love remove.
Affliction's fire is kindled for wond'rous good, we're told,
It burns the dross within us and purifies the gold.
Then on affliction's anvil my heart I'll place resigned,
Before God's loving hammer whose strokes are just and kind;
And when His blessed image is stamped upon my heart,
His love has joys immortal, forever to impart.
'Tis hard to conquer passions, to check the bitter sighs—
So hard to gain the vict'ry when angry murmurs rise:
But when, through grace, we're able to say: "Thy will be done,"
Entire acquiescence is Heaven here begun:
And when, in Love's fair Eden, we've joined the ransomed
        throng,
A retrospective vision shall wake the gladsome song:
For we shall see Earth's trials as min'st'ring Angels stand,
Who've served for our salvation with Wisdom hand in hand.

True Fortitude.

'Tis not the grand and lofty tree,
That swings its head in air,
That prides itself in branches green
And blossoms rich and fair—
That spreads itself in loudest boasts,
With stern, relentless will,
And scornes the fragrant shrubs and plants
That grace the little rill;
Though feeling most secure and safe
From ev'ry thought of harm,
'Tis not this giant best survives
The fury of the storm.
When tempests roar, and angry winds
Are raging all around,
Its stiff and stubborn head, soon crushed,
Falls shattered to the ground.
But see the little violet,
That blossoms at its base:
In modest, sweet humility,
It turns its little face
Right to the Earth, and hides itself
Until the storm is o'er;
Then lifts aloft its sweet blue head,
More lovely than before.
O, Virtue, of all virtue's gems,
Among the very best,
Securing peace in ev'ry storm,
In ev'ry conflict rest;

True fortitude this gem displays,
　　Submission is its name ;
It shines serene when skies are blue,—
　　In conflicts just the same.
Then learn a lesson of the grass :
　　To bend when winds are high—
To hide thyself on Jesus' breast
　　When gathering storms are nigh ;
And when the heavy rain is spent,
　　To look aloft once more,
Refreshed and purified and blest,
　　And stronger than before.
Life's storms must break our stubborn will,
　　Its tempests wild must roll,
To conquer pride and selfishness
　　That war against the Soul.
The heavy rains our Father sends
　　Are naught but showers of grace,
To purge the Soul, and thus restore
　　The image of his face.

Our Guiding Star.

This world were drear, yes, drear indeed,
　　Without a guiding star ;
And who hath not some star of hope
　　That sheds its beams afar,
To guide his feet, to light his path,
　　To cheer each gloomy day,
To brighten ev'ry onward step
　　Upon the toilsome way.

For some, the sorrows of this world
　　Have clouded life's bright day;
The darkness is so dense, they scarce
　　Discern one beaming ray.
And yet they feel that there must be
　　Some light that shines afar;
So trusting on, they hope again
　　To see their guiding star.

For some, the star of earthly bliss
　　Is beaming fair and bright;
And steeped in luxury and ease,
　　They bask within its light.
But though its beams illuminate
　　Their palace grand and fair,
True happiness and purest joys
　　Are seldom tasted there.

Some see the star of fair renown;
　　And guided by its glow,
They struggle on from morn till night
　　To gain their prize; and lo!
When they have reached the golden heights
　　Of fair renown and fame,
They find that happiness cannot
　　Be purchased with a name.

Some see the dazzle and the glow
　　Of bright and shining gold;
They think this glittering mass indeed
　　Can happiness unfold;

And to obtain their cherished store,
    Their lives, their all they bring;
But lo? their idol is but gold—
    A cold and lifeless thing.

Let others bask within the light
    Which seems most fair to them:
Our guiding star, Oh, let It be
    The Star of Bethlehem.
This Star, we know, will guide us safe
    To our eternal home,
Where this same Star is all the light—
    Where darkness cannot come.

True Beauty.

"Beautiful hands are those that do
    Work that is earnest, brave and true."
Beautiful feet are those that tread
    Only the path where Jesus led;
Beautiful fingers, weaving flow'rs
    To cheer the suff'rer's lonely hours;
Beautiful voices, those that sing
    Praises to Christ, our Lord and King;
Beautiful lips are those that move
    Only to speak a Saviour's love;
Beautiful eyes that turn from Earth
    To seek the things of Heav'nly birth;
Beautiful ears, that hearken well,
    To truths which Jesus came to tell;

Beautiful faces, those that shine
  With kindly smiles of love divine;
Beautiful brows, that wear the crown
  Of innocence' unstained renown;
Beautiful hearts, that choose for dress,
  Garments of purest holiness;
Beautiful lives, devoted thus,
  Living for Him who died for us.

The Roses are Here.

Thrice welcome the roses, the feast of the roses,
  The queen of the seasons, the pride of the year!
Come visit their bowers, and welcome the flowers
  That gladden the Earth with their beauty and cheer.
Behold in the morning, their freshness adorning
  The Earth in their whiteness, their crimson and gold;
What innocent pleasure, what joy beyond measure,
  In watching their beautiful petals unfold.

Come feast on the roses, while nature discloses
  Her wealth of luxuriant floral display;
Come taste of their sweetness, alas! in their fleetness,
  They brighten our pathway, then droop and decay.
O beautiful season, pray tell us the reason,
  Thy days are so fleeting and brief is thy stay!
Oh, why must they leave us—the roses—'twill grieve
      us,
  Oh, why must their freshness and beauty decay.

Ah, yes! they must perish, the roses we cherish;
. For they are but earthly; the scent they disclose
Is but a faint token of fragrance unbroken,
    They serve but as simbols of Sharon's fair Rose.
They teach in their duty and Heavenly beauty,
    Of Him Who's "The Life" and "The Truth" and
        "The Way";   ·
They point to the Bower made fair by that Flower—
Immortal, unfading, exempt from decay.

They tell in their fleetness and vanishing sweetness,
    How brief is the season of earthly delight;
All temporal pleasures, all Earth's golden treasures—
    They come and are gone like a dream in the night.
But, O, blest assurance! there's endless endurance
    In Sharon's fair Rose and His beauty divine;
His fragrance attending, breathes Life never-ending:
How sweet on this Rose-bed of Love to recline!

Ora et Labora.

We deem our efforts useless,
    Our toil is vain, we often say;
We cannot see the merit
    In toiling on from day to day.
We fail to note the power
    Of patient work and constant prayer;
And so we often murmur
    And yield to doubtings and despair.

Still, "Let us not be weary
 In doing good", but let us try
To fill each little moment
 As God appoints: and by-and-bye,
All loving acts of kindness
 Shall in our crown of glory shine
Like gems in Heavenly brightness—
 Like stars in radiance divine.

"Your works shall be rewarded:"
 Your kindly words, your acts of love,
Which you have long forgotten,
 Are written in God's book above.
There they shall tell the story
 Of patient toil and earnest prayer;
And what you've deemed but useless
 Shall shine in heavenly luster there.

"Your work shall be rewarded:"
 Oh, can you not believe His word?
Can you not trust his promise,
 And wait and labor for the Lord?
No act of love is useless,
 No work of charity too small;
But many wait for great ones,
 And thus neglect to serve at all.

We look beyond the duties
 Which lie within our path to-day;
How oft we pass the roses
 Which bloom along our onward way!

"Your work shall be rewarded:"
  Not only deeds of wondrous might,
But little acts for Jesus,
  Are just as pleasing in his sight.
He looks upon the spirit
  With which we serve from day to day;
'Tis His to add the blessing,
  'Tis mine to labor and to pray.

Edwina's First Birthday.

'Tis the nineteenth day of the beautiful May,
  And the year it is eighty and nine;
But was ever a day half so beauteous and gay?
  Did the sun e'er so brilliantly shine?
E'en the clouds that arise now and then in the skies,
  And at times, breaking forth from above,
Seem but shadows of joy in their happy employ,
  Keeping time with the beating of love.

But you're longing to know why the world is aglow,
  What occasions such gladness, you say:
Only listen, my dear, and the cause you shall hear:
  Isn't baby one year old to-day?
To the mother's fond heart, could one blessing impart
  More of pleasure, of comfort and pride?
Is there flower so rare, half so beauteous and fair
  As the rose-bud that plays at her side?

Could one note in the song of the birds' merry throng,
    Half so thrilling and musical be—
Half so charming and true as her baby's "Ah-goo",
    In her innocent prattle and glee?
Yes, her heart feels the love that a mother can prove,
    But her joy it is mingled with pain;
So her tears and her smile interchange all the while,
    Like the sunshine without and the rain.

For the mem'ry of one so beloved, who is gone,
    Who would share in her pleasure to-day,
Adds a low minor strain to the happy refrain
    Sadder made by the brightness of May.
But in baby's sweet face not one shadow we trace—
    Life's horizon for her is but blue;
All her pathway 'mid bow'rs of the fairest of flow'rs.
    And her joys all unchanging and true.

Yes, our wishes for thee, dear Edwina, shall be
    Even such as thy year's happy dream;
May the world truly prove such a garden of love,
    Ever fair with affection's bright beam.
May thy life daily grow in that fullness below,
    Which at last, all completed, shall shine
In that Beautiful Land, at the Saviour's right hand,
    In the fullness of rapture divine.

Aspiration.

Give me to seek my heart's delight
    In things that are above—
To walk by faith, though not by sight,
    Confiding in His love.

Thou Who dost hear the raven's cry,
    My feeble frame dost know;
Thou canst my daily wants supply
    And needful grace bestow.

Let me but strive arrayed to be
    In graces all divine;
Robed in the Lily's purity,
    In holiness to shine.

Give me a faith that knows no doubt,
    Whate'er my lot may be—
Sweet peace within, whate'er without—
    A child-like trust in Thee.

Sabbath Rest.

Sweet Sabbath day, O, day of rest,
    With Heaven's own benediction blessed,
From earthly care and labor free,
    We would refresh ourselves in Thee.

Sweet Sabbath day, thy shade we seek,
  O fair oasis of the week;
Thy cooling founts, how sweet the taste,
  To pilgrims in a desert waste.

Sweet Sabbath day, of days the best,—
  In holy service truly blest—
Oh, may no idle thought annoy
  Our holy duty, holy joy.

Sweet Sabbath day, oh, may it be
  A day of pleasure, Lord, in Thee!
A day of rest in works of love—
  A foretaste of the rest above.

'Tis a Picture on Memory's Wall.

"If you could only see!" Brother tenderly said,
  As he witnessed my joy and delight;
"Could you see it, ah, then you might truly enjoy
  And remember this beautiful sight!"

Could the mind not conceive its ideal designs—
  Might it not on the beautiful feed—
Then, alas! who could fathom our darkness and
    gloom!
  Then 'twere sad to be sightless, indeed.

To the physical eye—yes, it may be, perchance—
  It is fairer and lovelier still;

But the picture in mind of that floral repast
    Shall its place in my memory fill.

There is many a portrait of friendship and love
    Glowing brightly on memory's wall;
And to these there are added my garden delights,
    And the kindness they sweetly recall.

Oh, the clusters of flowers they placed in my hands,
    And the branches so fragrant and sweet!
How they made my return in the mild summer eve,
    With refreshment and gladness complete.

Yes, that beautiful, massive and tasteful bouquet,
    Breathing fragrance and friendship sincere,
Ever verdant and fresh in my mem'ry 'twill live
    With its perfume to gladden and cheer.

All throughout those bright days while it scented
      my room,
    Prompting many a beauteous design,
How it pointed my Soul to that Paradise fair
    With its roses and lilies divine.

And when Earth's bitter trials would darken my
      way
    With temptations of sadness and gloom,
I shall visit in fancy this garden once more,
    And shall feast on its fragrance and bloom.

'Twas a foretaste to me of that Garden above,
    Where life's pleasures unceasingly flow;
Where the Soul shall repose on its rosebed of
      love,
    And life's flowers unfadingly grow.

What We Mourn For.

Why that bell so sadly tolling!
  Has some loved one passed away
Into rest from Earthly labor,
  Promised joys and endless day?
Why then toll those mournful dirges?
  Should we not rejoice to know
That some faithful steward has finished
  His appointed work below?

Not for those "Asleep in Jesus"
  Need our doleful knell be rung;
Not for those who've wrought their mission,
  Need our mournful dirge be sung.
Rather let us mourn and sorrow
  For the living all around
Dead in trespasses, unmindful
  Of the Gospel's joyful sound.

There is death where life seems brightest;
  Death of all that's pure and good—
Of that higher life whose heart-throb
  Is true man- and woman-hood.
Yes, there's death among the living—
  Death of all that maketh life
Worthy of its stern endeavor,   ·
  Of its toils, its cross and strife.

Worthy of its destination
　　And its origin divine;—
Death of all those holy graces
　　Wherein every Soul should shine;—
Death of all that's best and noblest—
　　Of a self-denying love;
Death of holy aspirations—
　　Longings for the things above.

Ah, 'tis meet to mourn and sorrow
　　For the graves that round us rise—
Graves of blighted loves and friendships,
　　Shattered hopes and broken ties;
Resolutions all forgotten,
　　Promises but made in vain;
Golden dreams that had aspired
　　To the noblest to attain;
Virtue's lessons all unheeded,
　　Innocence and Mother's prayer,
Childhood scenes—all desecrated,—
　　All lie dead and buried there.

Here is death in all its horror—
　　Here is cause for grief sincere;
Lo! the monster in his blackness,
　　Void of comfort, void of cheer.

Sound the resurrection trumpet
　　Over him who fails to see
Life in its exalted purpose,
　　Loveliness and purity;—

Over him who gropes in darkness
  'Mid the ills of mortal life,
Heart-sick with its disappointments,
  Its vicissitudes and strife.

Oh, that such might be awakened
  From the death of mortal gloom,
To the Life of endless brightness,
  Teeming with immortal bloom.

True Friendship.

Hast thou tasted of its sweetness?
  Dost thou know its precious worth?
Hast thou learned that of the flowers
  Blossoming upon the earth
Friendship's roses are the fairest?—
  That their rare and sweet perfume
Serves to brighten all life's pathway
  And to charm away its gloom?

Hast thou felt its magic power
  When the heart is sore oppressed?—
When life's cares and stern endeavors
  Caused a longing in the breast
For some hand to lift the burden—
  For a kind and loving voice
To revive thy drooping spirits—
  Bid thy fainting heart rejoice?

Ah, in time of deepest trouble,
   In bereavement's tearful hour,
Who can estimate its value?—
   Who can speak its healing pow'r?
Yes, the gift of changeless friendship
   Is a rare and priceless gem;
Far more precious than the diamonds
   In a royal diadem.

'Tis the golden chain that bindeth
   Heart to heart and Soul to Soul;
'Tis the chain that naught can sever
   While life's changeful seasons roll.
Charms of youth and health and beauty—
   These may share misfortune's blight;
But the golden links of friendship
   Gleam more radiant and bright.

Fortune's splendor, fame and glory—
   What are these in time of grief?
Can they soothe our throbbing temples?—
   Can they bring the heart relief?
Ah, no! 'Tis the touch of friendship
   That must charm away our pain;
'Tis the voice of friend or loved one
   That must wake the soothing strain

Which can hush the angry billows
   That are heaving in the breast;
Nothing else can calm the tempest
   And restore the heart's true rest;

Friendship true, sincere and faithful,
  Knows no wavering, feels no ill;
Though the stars should cease their shining,
  It is changeless friendship still.

Storms of life may beat in fury,
  Troubles come, and fortunes fall;
But the holy star of friendship
  Shines serenely through it all.
Life's adversities may gather;
  Clouds may darken all the way,
But the light of holy friendship
  Turns the darkness into day.

But whence springs this holy friendship?
  Is it common to mankind?
Is it freely spent, and always
  With a sacred trust enshrined?
No! ah, no! 'Tis rarely tender'd,
  'Tis a gift that's from above;
'Tis the love our Master taught us—
  Love divine, unchanging love.

The Rose.

Queen of beauty, royal mistress
  Of all Nature's gems;
Fairer than the pearls adorning
  Kingly diadems!

For it breathes the choicest fragrance
    From its Maker's hand,
And it points us in its mission
    To the Better Land.

In its innocence and beauty,
    With its sweet perfume,
It delights and cheers the suff'rer
    In his lonely room.
Though his eyes so dim and weary,
    Turn from things of Earth,
They will recognize this flower
    Of celestial birth.

On the lowly mound it blossoms,
    Where the Christian sleeps;
And reminds the sad bereaved one
    As he stands and weeps,
That the Spirit of his loved one
    'Bides not in that tomb,
But in living beauty riseth
    Like the sweet perfume.

Do thou, like the rose, dear reader,
    Comfort, cheer and bless,
And array thyself in beauty
    In the Saviour's dress.
Breathe the fragrance of his presence
    Wheresoe'er thou art,
Let the savor of His sweetness
    Flow from out thy heart.

Make thy mission pure and holy,
　Like this lovely rose;
It does naught but cheer and comfort
　Wheresoe'er it goes.
It fulfills its holy calling,
　And its Maker's will;
Learn its mission dear beloved one,
　And thine own fulfill.

~ ~ ~ ~ ~

Within the Vale.

Art thou weary, dear reader, discouraged and sad,
　Doth it seem that thy life is but vain --
Since thy lot hath so lowly and humbly been cast
　That thy light must unheeded remain?
Oh, remember He loves us and tenderly cares,
　Who assigneth thy mission and mine ;
And no doubt 'tis just here, in the vale dark and lone,
　He most needeth our faith-gleams to shine.

Not in beautiful gardens where roses abound,
　May the pansy best service impart ;
But alone on the desert, surrounded by waste,
　How it cheers the faint traveler's heart !
And the dear little stars--how they vanish to naught
　In the glorious dazzle of day !
It is only the darkness can teach us the worth
　Of their tiny but exquisite ray.

Doth it seem, too, dear friend, that no virtue can dwell
　In the midst of such guilt and such gloom !--
That no graces can thrive 'mid surroundings so drear,
　But must lose all their beauty and bloom ? -

Oh, then note what a lesson the Psalmist implies
　　When alluding to records of old,
Where we read of the beautiful, innocent doves
　　Making oft their abode, we are told,

In the nooks of the tiling, where people were wont
　　All their refuse and litter to throw.
Here they dwelt in the crevices, washed by the rains,
　　In the midst of the rubbish ; and lo !
Is their beauty and innocence marred by the dregs?
　　Is their purity less than before?
Are they doves any less, or their plumage less bright,
　　As aloft through the sunlight they soar?

Ah, no ! For their wings are as silvery gems,
　　And their feathers as sprinkled with gold.
Little question with them where the night hath been spent,
　　When at morn their white wings they unfold.
What a comforting lesson, reviving and sweet !
　　For whatever our station— 'tis He
Yea, the Lamb that was slain— shall our Souls ever cleanse,
　　And their beauty and innocence be.

Oh, 'tis blest to be guided and kept by His hand ;
　　So whatever the world hath in store,
'Neath His own mighty wings he will shelter our Souls
　　Till the time of probation is o'er.
Little matters it then what our Earthly abode,
　　When the Soul shall have taken its flight,
And in robes of His Righteousness, spotless and pure,
　　Shall have entered the City of Light.

Taste and be Satisfied.

Athirst and weary, long I strayed,
Where naught my burning thirst allayed;
Naught that my burning lips would try
Could e'er the cooling drops supply.
"Come where the Living Waters flow,"
I heard Him say in accents low;
And drawing close to Jesus' side,
My thirsty Soul was satisfied.

A hungry pilgrim faint and cold,
I wandered long without the fold;
Far from the tender Shepherd's care,
From shady rills and pastures fair.
"I am the Bread, the Living bread,"
A voice divine in mercy said:
And pressing on to Jesus' side,
The Manna sweet His grace supplied.

With Soul benighted and dismay'd,
Long in the paths of sin I stray'd:
With ev'ry onward step, I knew,
More dense and deep the darkness grew.
"I am the Light," I heard Him say,
"Return, O wanderer, from thy way!"
And coming straight to Jesus' side,
His tender Love the Light supplied.

The Giver of All Good Gifts.

Every perfect gift decendeth
  From the Father of all Light,
Whose eternal day of glory
  Knows no shadow of the night.
Light and joy and peace and gladness—
  All are sent from God above,
Streams of blessings ever flowing
  From the fountain of his love.

His, the gift of golden sunshine,
  In its radiance warm and bright;
His, the stars that shine so brightly,
  To illuminate our night.
Ev'ry flower, ev'ry dewdrop—
  Sparkling in the morning sun,
Timely rains and cooling showers—
  Are His free gifts, every one.

Hast thou ought which was not freely
  Of the Father sent to thee?
All thy comforts and thy blessings
  Are His gifts so full and free;
His, thy riches and thy talents—
  All thy stores and all thy wealth;
His, the gift of all thy treasures—
  His, the gift of life and health.

Is thy glad heart full of sunshine?
   Then remember, 'tis from God;
Scatter it along thy pathway,
   That thy light may shine abroad,
To direct some weary wand'rer
   Back to Him, the source of light;
Think how much of good may follow
   If thy path be always bright.

"Let your light so shine" that others
   May be guided by its rays
Into paths of truth and virtue—
   Into brighter, better ways;
Let thy joy and gladness teach them
   That the Father of all light
Makes the lives of those who love Him
   Always happy, always bright.

Hast thou sorrow? then remember
   Naught of ill can come from Him;
Bright and warm His love is burning,
   'Tho' thy lamp of joy burn dim.
All that comes from Him is blessed,
   Be it joy, or be it pain;
Naught of ill can harm His children
   For His love and care remain.

On the darkest cloud that gathers,
   If submissive to His will,
We can see God's loving rainbow
   Shining forth His goodness still.

Murmurings must cease within us,
  And our grateful bosom swell
With thanksgiving joys; for surely
  He doth order all things well.

Art thou blessed with earthly treasures?
  Use them in the Master's name;
Help to spread the glorious Gospel,
  And the Saviour's love proclaim.
Use them to uplift the fallen—
  To supply the orphans' need;
To remove the thorns of Satan,
  And to scatter Heavenly seed.

Many precious Souls are dying,
  Calling for thy speedy aid;
All around thee pant for comfort
  Hearts so weary and dismayed.
Use the riches God has given
  To promote His blessed cause;
Helping others, thou dost serve Him
  And obey His holy laws.

Hast thou talents?—then remember
  They are of thy Father's hand—
Gifts entrusted to thy keeping,
  Which His justice shall demand
With a rich and goodly increase;
  They are His—they are not thine—
Thou shalt purchase with them jewels
  In the Saviour's crown to shine.

Give to others of the blessings
 Which He gave so full and free;—
In proportion as thou givest
 Shall His blessing flow on thee.
Talents shine with brighter luster
 In as much as they are used;
Every gift that God has given
 Should be cherished, not abused.

Hast thou many friends and loved ones,
 Who have cheered and blessed thy days—
Who have scattered friendship's roses
 All along thy varied ways?
Then be grateful, but remember
 Jesus is thy truest friend—
Sticking closer than a brother—
 Leading, loving to the end.

Hast thou parents, brothers, sisters,
 And a bright and happy home?
Then remember with compassion
Sad ones who are left to roam.
 Do not close thy door upon them,
Bless them in their hour of need;
 By a word or act of kindness,
Thou canst prove their friend indeed.

Yes, thy gifts, they all are sent thee,
 From the Father, kind and true;
E'en his well-beloved Jesus
 Was a gift He sent to you.

Should not such a gracious Father
  In his well-beloved Son,
Freely give His children all things
  If they but his mercies own?

Who can measure, who can fathom
  Love so tender, so divine!
Can I estimate the treasures
  Which in Jesus Christ are mine?
No, ah! no; I can but love Him,
  Can but worship and adore;
Can but touch upon his goodness,
  Tho' I tell it o'er and o'er.

How I long to sing His praises!—
  Long to sing his wondrous love,
With the Seraphim and Angels
  And the Cherubim above!
Who in strains of sweetest music,
  All His gifts and works adore,
Singing "Holy!" "Holy!" "Holy,"
  Blessed Lord for evermore.

A Golden Wedding.

Hark, their sweet melodious ringing,
　Golden Wedding Bells!
And with fancy backward drifting,
　How their music tells
Of a glad December morning,
When the rosy dawn gave warning
That before another sun
Two glad hearts should be as one.

See the happy youth and maiden—
　Thrilling hearts aglow;
All the fair and sunny Southland
　Seems one heaven below;
Faithful hearts in love united,
Marriage vows sincerely plighted—
Hand in hand, and side by side,
Stately youth and blushing bride.

Half a century has vanished
　Golden Wedding Bells;
And how wonderful the story
　Which their music tells!
How it tell of joys and sorrows!
Sad to-days and glad to-morrows!
How it tells of hopes and fears,
Toils and struggles, smiles and tears!

Fifty years of union service—
  What a record fair;
How it weaves its beauteous chaplet
  Wreathing silver hair!
And on heads now bowed and hoary,
Fairer far that wreath of glory,
Than the Orange Blooms of snow,
On that day of long ago.

Looking back upon the pathway
  Of so many years,
How the scene, oft strangely varied,
  Wakes both smiles and tears!
There beside the cypress drooping,
Pleasures' roses, too, are grouping:—
Now the valley dark with gloom,
Now the mount of light and bloom.

Still two hearts in loving union,
  Shared their joys and griefs;
And to every care that burden'd
  Love brought sweet relief.
Year by year has swiftly glided,
Joys more sweet because divided;
And with willing hearts to share,
Toils and cares more light to bear.

Six glad mornings brought their tidings
  From the natal room;
Making sunshine in the homestead—
  Banishing all gloom.

Parent hearts in fond emotion,
Bubbling o'er with pure devotion;
Planning pleasures, tracing ways,
For their darlings' future days.

But, alas! three sad occasions
    Draped the home in gloom;
When the precious forms of loved ones
    Sank within the tomb.
But the same Lord who had given,
Called His own again to Heaven;
And, in life and death the same,
"Blessed be His holy name."

Parents dear, beloved and honored,
    We whom God hath spared,
We who long your tender kindness,
    Long your love have shared,
Fain to-day our dues would offer—
Fain some worthy tribute proffer;
But we've naught our thanks to prove—
Naught but gratitude and love.

Still we pray that Heaven's blessings
    May your path attend,
And each coming day grow brighter
    To the journey's end.
Truly all your kindness tendered—
Ev'ry noble action rendered,
Yea, each word and deed of love
Bears its record Home above.

There a rich reward shall meet you,
  When your race is run;
There our blessed Lord shall greet you,
  With His sweet "Well done."
To that throne of snowy whiteness
May your outlook grow in brightness,
And each Earthly joy more sweet,
Till it ends in joys complete.

May your good life's sun shine brightest
  Sinking in the West,
And its evening shades while blending,
  Bring eternal rest.
Happy then with Christ your meeting,
When your Soul shall catch the greeting,
"Come and lay your trophies down,
And receive your starry crown."

Evening Tribute.

"A day's march nearer Home,"
  "O, sweetly solemn thought!"
And yet I mourn that I this day
  So little good have wrought.
I would do more for Thee,
  My Father and my God;
Thy goodness I would fain proclaim
  Through all the world abroad.

For Thou hast safely led
  Me on from childhood's hour;
Through all my life Thy love hast shown,
  And Thy protecting pow'r;
My pathway Thou hast strewn
  With roses of success,
And many friends Thou givest me,
  My life to cheer and bless.

For all these mercies, Lord,
  Which hourly I meet,
My grateful heart would something bring
  To lay down at Thy feet;
Some tribute, dearest Lord,
  I fain would bring to Thee;
Some word of praise, some act of love,
  For all Thy love to me.

But ah, too well I know
  That I have nothing meet
To bring before a sovereign God
  Who is in all complete:
But here's my grateful heart;
  Take it and make it Thine;
And grant that through my future life
  A brighter light may shine,—

That those around may see
  How good and kind thou art—
The light and joy Thou givest me
  I would to them impart;

Help me to use the gifts
   And talents I possess,
To glorify Thy holy name
   And other lives to bless;—
Some Soul to win for Thee,

Some lonely heart to cheer,
Some sob to still, some smile renew,
   Or stay the gath'ring tear;
That when my Soul is called
   From Earth to Heav'n above,
I may not come with empty hands,
   But bring some fruit of love.

Recompense.

And is it worth the living,
   This life so full of cares,
So full of sore temptations,
   So full of tempters' snares,
So full of disappointments,
   Of shatter'd hopes and ties,
So full of toils and struggles,
   Of bitter sobs and sighs,
So full of sad bereavements,
   Of heart-aches and of pain—
Where ev'ry Christmas carol
   Must have its sad refrain?—

Ah, yes! 'tis worth the living,
    This precious life of ours;
Among its thorns and thistles
    There bloom the sweetest flowers.

For ev'ry sore temptation
    There is sufficient grace,
From ev'ry foe and tempter
    There is a hiding place.

For ev'ry wound of sorrow
    There is a healing balm;
And with each storm of trouble
    There comes a peaceful calm.

From ev'ry care that burdens,
    From ev'ry bitter grief,
Love's peaceful benediction
    Brings sure and sweet relief.

For ev'ry loved one taken
    To dwell with Him above,
Another tie is added—
    Another cord of love.

To draw us to the region
    Where all is peace and joy,
Where sorrows never enter,
    And cares no more annoy.

And for the cross that grieves us—
    Its hard and earnest strife—
A starry crown is offer'd
    Of "Everlasting Life".

The obstacles and trials
    Which ev'rywhere we meet,
Are stepping-stones to Heaven,
    To guide our wand'ring feet.

The sigh must wake the longing
　　For better things above,
Afflictions and bereavements
　　Must purify our love;
Life's bitter disappointments
　　Must wake that thirst within,
Which seeks the "Living Water"
　　To quench the fire of sin;
The Soul's dissatisfaction,
　　Its never-ending strife,
Its hungerings and cravings
　　Must seek the "Bread of Life";
The longings and the strivings
　　Which stir within the breast,
Must grasp the invitation,
　　"Come, I will give you rest."
This world cannot afford us
　　The things for which we sigh,
So we must look above it
　　And draw them from on high.
Then blest be all life's trials
　　Which bring us to our Lord,
Since He has kindly promised
　　For all a sweet reward.

Love's Tribute.

'Tis the fragrant month of roses,
    Fairest season of the year;
'Tis the fifth of June, and listen!
    Bells are ringing sweet and clear,
Calling men to Sabbath worship—
    But has not their silvery chime
Something more than usual sweetness?
    Does it not recall the time
Of a happy, blest occasion,
    Five-and-twenty years ago,
When the world was all an Eden
    For two happy hearts aglow?
Sweeter roses, fairer lilies
    Never kissed a brighter sun;
For the Orange Blooms had told them
    Of two loving hearts made one:
Fannie Bell with Ernest Marshall,
    Hand in hand and side by side—
Handsome youth and blooming maiden—
    Stately groom and lovely bride.
Fortune's smile has hovered o'er them:
    Ev'ry morn sent blessings new;
Friends and kindred—none but cherish
    Hearts so noble kind and true.
Of the fair quartette of children,
    One was early called above,

Where her voice is sweetly blending
In the chords of endless love:
Far too gentle, too angelic
To resist Earth's storms and strife—
Tender blossom, fitted only
For the bloom of Heav'nly life.
And the trio that remaineth—
May their lives a blessing prove!
May their concord be unbroken
Till they, too, are called above!
Over him in far Alaska,
We beseech God's mighty pow'r
To protect and safe return him,
In His own appointed hour.
Five-and-twenty years have glided
"Gently down the stream of time,"
And to-day, while bells are ringing
Forth the Silver Wedding chime,
From the far-extended circle
Of devoted friends, there come
Words of fond congratulation
To the happy Marshall home.
Rock Hill Church bequeaths its blessing,
Rock Hill School its grateful love;
The community of Windom—
Friends and neighbors—all would prove
Their devotion to the family
That has ever firmly stood,
Noble-minded, kindly-hearted,
And dispensing naught but good.
Friends beloved, esteemed and cherished,
May your future life, we pray,

Heaven's choicest benedictions
    Realize from day to day,
To this Silver anniversary
    May the Golden add its seal!—
Yea, the Diamond—if it please Him
    Who dispenseth life and weal.
And when clouds your sky o'ershadow
    And would hide its sunlight fair,
May you see their "Silver Lining"
    And God's "Bow of Promise" there.
'Tis the wish of true affection,
    'Tis our heartfelt tribute given;
We but tender our devotions,
    Leaving all the rest to Heaven.

Evening Meditation.

The birds have sung His praises;
    Have spent the day in worshipping;
Have cheered the world about them,
    And made the woods with music ring.
They've brought their grateful tribute
    To their Creator's holy name—
In merry tuneful warbles
    They've sung His love and told His fame.

The roses and the lilies
    Have taught His purity and grace;
Reflecting in their beauty
    Bright visions from their Maker's face.

They've honored Him and served Him;
   Have freely spent their sweet perfume
To cheer the lonely suff'rer
   And charm away his pain and gloom.

The merry, playful sunbeams
   Have deemed it but a sweet delight,
O'er ev'ry stream and meadow
   To pour their bright and sparkling light.
All Nature has been faithful
   In its appointed sphere to shine;
The smallest plants and blossoms
   Have taught some attribute divine.

But what hast thou been doing,
   O, Soul of mine? Hast thou been true
To thine appointed mission?
   Hast thou been eager to pursue
The path of holy duty,
   Of purity and righteousness?
Hast thou advanced in virtue,
   In Godly life and growth of grace?

Hast thou employed thy talents
   Thine own good mission to fulfill—
To honor thy Creator,
   And do thy Father's holy will?
To use each golden moment
   For its appointed act of love,
Whose merit has ascended
   For Angels to record above?

Hast thou with Nature blended
  In one harmonious chord of praise
To Him whose love and mercy
  Have showered blessings on thy ways?
Or hast thou been neglectful
  Of thine appointed work of God—
Forgetful of thy mission
  To spread His love and fame abroad?
Hast thou but used thy talents
  Some cherished idol to attain,
And spent thy "Pound" intrusted
  For selfish pleasures, worldly gain?
Ah, yes, dear Lord, I'm mindful
  That I have naught to bring to Thee,
But sad neglect and failure
  In works and gifts intrusted me.
O, blessed consolation!
  Thy love is ev'ry morning new,
Thy mercy is unbounded;
  Thy Father heart unchanging, true.
A book of snowy whiteness
  Is spread before my wond'ring gaze,
In which to try new records,
  Forgetful of departed days.
Then up, my Soul! Take courage!
  Press forward with an earnest will,
Strive with a brighter record,
  The pages of that book to fill.
Let ev'ry glowing sunset,
  While lighting up the Western sky,
Record some worthy action
  Accomplish'd in the day gone by;

And thus each rosy sunrise
  Will spread before thy wand'ring view,
New fields of precious labor,
  Still nobler work for thee to do.

Birthday Greeting.

Should the day prove dark and dreary,
  Clouded o'er with shades of night,
Void of ev'ry Earthly pleasure—
  Void of sunbeams fair and bright—
Let thine heart no trouble borrow!
There is One who knows thy sorrow,
And Who sweetly speaks to thee,
"As thy day thy strength shall be."

Should the day bring grief and trouble,
  More, 'twould seem, than thou canst bear,
More than Earthly friends or kindred—
  More than human love can share—
Still divinest Light is streaming
And a "Bow of Promise" gleaming,
In His precious words to thee:
"As thy day thy strength shall be."

Should the day be full of sunshine,
  Bringing joy and pleasures gay,
Shedding light upon thy pathway,
  Strewing flow'rs along thy way,

Oh, then, drink thy cup of gladness,
Banishing all thoughts of sadness,
In that all-sufficient plea:
"As thy day thy strength shall be."

Not to me, dear friend, 'tis given
　　Light or shade to wish for thee;
For the Father only knoweth
　　Which of these the best may be;
But I pray His love to guide thee,
And from storms of ill to hide thee;
That in all He sendeth thee
"As thy day thy strength shall be."

The Coronet of Years.

Shall it shine in Heav'nly beauty
　　In the silver'd hair,
When thy head is bowed and hoary,
　　Shall it glisten there?

Free from stain and free from blemish,
　　Like a radiant star,
Sending down the track of ages
　　Rays to shine afar?

Pointing out the path of duty
　　To another's feet—
Pointing out the way to honor
　　And to joys complete?

Oh! then, use each golden moment!
  Let each day be set
Like a fair and priceless jewel
  In this Coronet.

Ev'ry day of loving service
  Adds a precious gem
That shall glitter in the splendor
  Of this diadem.

But each idle, ill-spent moment
  Mars its beauty rare;
Yea, each moment of ill-doing
  Leaves its guilt stain there.

And thy loving guardian angels
  Shed their silent tears,
As they strive to hide each blemish
  In the crown of years.

The Beautiful.

The Universe bespeaks it
  In countless forms and matchless hues—
Creation's map reveals it
  In symmetry of shapes and views.
The azure dome above us,
  Bespangled with the stars at night,
The sunset in its glory,
  Serene and beautiful and bright—

The rosy light of morning
　That sparkles in the pearly dew,
The breaking cloud when painted
　In all the rainbow's richest hue—
The flowers fresh and fragrant
　In varied tints and scent and form,
The verdant fields and meadows,
　The cheery sunbeams bright and warm,
The myriad forms of beauty
　That in Creation's atlas shine—
All, all reflect the glory
　And attributes of Love divine.
'Tis Love that paints the lily
　And gives the rose its odor rare—
That prompts the lark to warble,
　The bob-o'-link to soar in air—
That paints the shining plumage
　Of ev'ry bird in ev'ry clime—
That beautifies Creation
　With loveliness and grace sublime.
Yet Love's unrivaled beauty
　Shines not in Nature's choicest dress,
But in the Soul's perfection—
　In purity and righteousness.

Our Hero Band.

God bless the brave and noble band
Who've left Columbia's peaceful strand—
Have dared to face the stormy sea,
For Cuba's weal and liberty—

Who've gone to succor and to bless
Our neighbor in her sad distress;
"For God and home and every land,"
Our motto for our hero band.

Protect them, O, Almighty Hand,
Who've breathed farewell to native land,
To home and wife and prattling child,
For cannon's roar and billows wild—
Not for the love of wealth or fame,
Of laurels fair, or hero's name—
"For God and home and ev'ry land,"
The impulse of our hero band.

All honor to the noble band,
Who've taken their decided stand
For justice, liberty and right;
For freedom from oppression's might;
And when o'er Cuba's peaceful isle
Glad freedom's light shall sweetly smile—
Safe to Columbia's happy land,
May Heav'n restore our hero band.

Be multiplied, O noble band,
In ev'ry age and ev'ry land,
Who battle manfully and strong
'Gainst all oppression, vice and wrong;
Who bear the tidings of "Good will"
O'er ocean wide, o'er plain and hill,
Till Freedom's banner wave unfurled
In love and peace o'er all the world.

The Light is Come.

Behold the fair and rosy dawn!
  Bright herald of the day,
Dispelling all the clouds and mists
  On its advancing way.
It tells of the retreating night,
And heralds the approaching Light.

Jesus "The Light," "The Life," "The Way"—
  That Light is dawning now;
Behold, a Heav'nly halo beams
  Around His infant brow.
A Light is risen on the Earth;—
'Tis breaking with the Saviour's birth.

It streams from out a manger low,
  Where on an humble bed
Of hay and moss, the Saviour deigns
  To lay His kingly head.
Oh, come and worship at the shrine
From which there beams such love divine!

It comes to guide us with its rays
  To endless bliss and joy;
It comes all shades of sin and death—
  All darkness to destroy.
It comes to banish all the gloom
And make the desert places bloom.

The Christ is born—our Christmas Joy—
  The King of kings is come;
He brings salvation, life and peace
  Down from His Heav'nly home.
The Christ is born: The Light divine
Is come in ev'ry heart to shine.

O, precious Light, we hail thy dawn,
  We need Thy Heav'nly pow'rs;
We need the sunshine of Thy love
  In these poor hearts of ours.
Without Thee, life indeed were sad,
With Thee, the humblest may be glad.

O, Gift of God, O, Saviour dear,
  To Thee our voice we raise
In Christmas anthems full of joy,
  Of gratitude and praise;
To Thee be endless glory given
By all on Earth and all in Heaven.

Christmas Sunshine.

The Christmas bells are ringing;
  Let men take up the joyful strain—
Devotion's tribute bringing,
  In Christmas carols' sweet refrain.

Commemorate with gladness
  The dawning of an era bright

Which burst the clouds of sadness
    And brought rejoicing Truth to light.

Life sweet and never-ending,
    Truth, Love and Immortality,
With purest joys attending,
    Are gifts it brought to you and me.

Man in the Soul's perfection—
    How high exalted and how great!—
His Maker's own reflection,
    And life and honor his estate.

Sin, sickness, pain and sorrow,
    However real these may seem,
Are but the ills we borrow—
    Are all but transient, all a dream.

Then why not quickly banish
    The thoughts of evil, death and pain!
Since these must duly vanish,
    And life and peace forever reign.

A Universe of beauty,
    Which moves in harmony divine,
Fulfilling holy duty,
    Is your abiding place and mine.

Here no discordant error,
    But harmony and peace serene—
One vast harmonious mirror
    Reflecting loveliness unseen.

Its teachings pure and holy,
  Bespeak the beautiful and good—
Sublime instructions solely
  Prescribed for man- and woman-hood.

Consider in its whiteness
  The little snowflake light in air;
A hexigon of brightness,
  Divinely wrought, exquisite, fair.

Its symmetry and beauty,
  Its emblematic purity,
Do these not speak of duty,
  In gentle terms to you and me?

The summer sunbeams dancing,
  O'er wood and meadow, hill and dale;
The moon and star-gems glancing,
  That decorate the night's dark veil;

The lilies and the roses,
  The violet's sweet, exquisite grace—
Such beauty but discloses
  The smile of our Creator's face;

And we, His own reflection,
  Should we not His effulgence prove?—
Not in the Soul's perfection
  Reveal His attributes of love?

Ah, yes! We'll soar in Spirit,
  The mortal things of Earth above,
And rightfully inherit
  Our legacy of Truth and Love.

And thus we'll join the chorus
   Of universal joy and praise?
And with Love's banner o'er us,
   We'll chant throughout eternal days

The gladsome natal story
   Of Him Who taught our Soul the way
To shine in endless glory,
   In beauty's dress and Love's array.

Merry Christmas to All.

Again they are ringing— so cheerily ringing--
   Sweet Christmas bells, chiming the story of old ;
And sweeter and better grows Bethlehem's story,
   As over and over its tidings are told.
Behold the great light that o'erwhelms the meek shepherds
   While guarding their flocks on that joy-bringing night !
To whom and for whom is the glad revelation,
   And whence are the beams of its radiance bright ?

The sweet, blending chords from multitude voices,
   Their choice benediction, their message of love
To whom and of whom is the theme of their rapture,
   And whence the sweet music poured out from above?
"On Earth" be the "peace"—canst thou hear, weary pilgrim ?
   "On Earth," not in Heaven—"On Earth" be the "peace,"
For Earth will be Heaven when "peace" shall pervade it,
   When discord and turmoil forever shall cease.

"Toward men" the "good will". Canst thou hear, weary
   pilgrim ?
Oh, turn but thine ear to that song from above !

The note ringing sweetest throughout the grand chorus,
That note is the note of immutable love,
'Tis thine, the great legacy! thine all the blessing!
'Tis thine, weary pilgrim, oh, list to the song!
"Toward men" the "good will". Then rejoice in thy fortune,
Chime in with the angels in notes full and strong!

That Star in the East over Bethlehem's manger!
Behold how it smiles on thy pathway and mine!
Its beams ever tender, its light ever real,
Undimmed by the ages its lustre divine.
O, love unalloyed! Perfect love, never ending —
Immortal, unchangeable, matchless and sweet!
"To God in the Highest" - Ah, this is the keynote
That preludes the song with such gladness complete

"To God" be the "glory," to Him the great Giver,
The Fount of all good and the source of our joy,
The Gift of His Love, be the theme of our anthem,
Let angels and men all their praises employ:
For sweet and consoling is Gabriel's story,
"Fear not", but rejoice in the tidings I bring:
"To you there is born, in the City of David, .
A Saviour", a Shepherd, Redeemer and King.

Like wise men of old let us open our treasure,
Our hearts and our lives be the gifts we unfold,
Our thoughts and our deeds, yea, the pulse of our being,
Be these our frankincense, our myrrh and our gold.

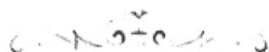

Easter Lilies.

Easter lilies—how they glisten
  In their robes of spotless white;
All arrayed in snowy whiteness,
How they sparkle in the brightness
  Of the Easter morning light.

How they lift their graceful petals,
  And in gladness seem to say:
We have burst the clods that bound us,
And delight in shedding round us
  Fragrance on this Easter day.

We've aspired to the sunshine
  That dispels the winter's gloom;
We have left our earth-walled prison—
Burst our shackles, and have risen
  Into beauty, light and bloom.

Wouldst thou join the happy chorus
  Of the Easter lilies' song?
Wouldst thou know the theme and glory
Of the resurrection story,
  And thine Easter joys prolong?

Then arise in joy, dear reader,
  Banish ev'ry thought of gloom!
Truth has triumphed over error,
Perfect love o'er slavish terror,
  Life immortal o'er the tomb.

Life is real, Truth is power,
  Love divine is all in all;
Mortal life is but a seeming—
A delusion and a dreaming—
  Hearken to the Spirit's call!

Rouse thee from the sleep of Adam,
  Which would all thy pow'rs enslave,
Which would helplessly confine thee,
And the spell which would resign thee
  To the darkness of the grave.

Rouse thee to the truth of being!
  Let thy Easter anthem be:
Resurrection—out of sadness
Into beauty, life and gladness—
  Into love's own liberty.

Don the snowy robes of spirit,
  Pure and beautiful and bright!
Truth and love in Christ confessing,
Claim the resurrection blessing
  Through His merit brought to light.

Break the spell of mortal seeming!
  And thy song of life shall be:
"Risen from the tomb of error,
Death where is thy sting of terror?
  Grave where is thy victory!"

Our Resurrection Chorus.

Triumphant, victorious o'er death and the tomb!
Light, light after darkness, and joy after gloom!
The bursting of shackles! the captives go free!
"Unfettered"! the motto henceforward shall be.

All nature rejoiceth in Easter delight:
While doffing her garments of wintery night,
She dons her habiliment verdant and fair,
Making beauteous the landscape and fragrant the air.

The fresh budding flowers, the leaves of new birth,
The warbling wing'd minstrels that gladden the earth;
The verdure beneath and the azure above,
The scenes all about us of gladness and love.

All, all are inviting the heart to rejoice,
And join in the chorus with jubilant voice.
Then who would be mournful, ah, who could be sad
In the midst of surroundings so cheery and glad?

The Saviour is risen, and with Him we soar
Into newness of life where we sorrow no more
The life with its beautiful mission of love,
The life that unceasingly draws from above

Its strength, its supplies, and its sunshine of joy
Which the world cannot give, nor can ever destroy:
The life leading outward of selfish design,
And into the secrets of wisdom divine,

That finds its delight in another's success,
That seeks but to elevate, comfort and bless,

Translating earth's discord, its turmoil and strife,
Into harmony sweet, yea, the concord of life :

That soars above common things, pelf and unrest,
That aspires to the highest, the noblest and best
The life ever rising and reaching above,
Till it loses itself in the ocean of love.

The Saviour is risen, thus bringeth to light
The life everlasting, immortal and bright.
Yes, the Saviour is risen, and with Him we rise
To the Eden of Love, the sweet home in the skies.

Light and Shade.

"The wall must wear the weather stain
    Before the ivy wreath."
Such is the thought expressed in rhyme,
Which bards and seers of every clime
    To rythmic lore bequeath.

Yes, we may trace the weather stain
    Beneath the myrtle green;
And roses that bedeck the vine
And gracefully our homes entwine,
    Are lined with thorns between.

No crown inlaid with jewels fair
    Without the cross, they say;
No break of morn, no rosy light,
But tells of the retreating night
    And darkness passed away.

No royal road, no flowery path
  Prescribe the way of life;
No chaplet fair, no laurels won,
No sweet reward for work well done,
  Without the toil and strife.

Rest comes with glad attainment's hour:
  The struggle goes before;
Choice erudition's diadem,
How dearly purchased, gem by gem,
  From Wisdom's precious store.

Thus joy and sorrow, light and shade,
  Each other's steps pursue;
To-day upon the shining height,
To-morrow in the vale of night—
  An ever changing view.

And yet is not life's checkered web
  The work of mortal mind?
Man, tracing out his own dark fate—
Outcome of his untutored state,
  Erroneous, faulty, blind?

The Giver of all perfect good
  Can naught of ill bestow;
From that benignant Fount above
Naught but a stream of boundless love
  And perfect good can flow.

The mind that's stayed on Love divine,
  Is kept in perfect peace;
It soars above all things of time,

It lives in harmony sublime
   And joys that never cease.

Life's panorama, dark or gay,
   Is by ourselves designed;
Some see the light and some the shade—
The varied aspects round us made
   Are pictures of the mind.

Our low conception 'tis that frames
   The form of sombre hue;
The shadow and the ills designed
Are phantoms of the human mind—
   Deceptive, void, untrue.

The soul in its effulgency
   Sees not the shades of gloom;
Encircled by eternal light,
It sees the beautiful and bright,
   The flow'ring and the bloom;

It sees the real and the good,
   The perfect and the true;
The beauteous forms of Love's design—
Resplendent, changeless and divine—
   Love's own reflected hue.

In ev'ry dewdrop it discerns
   The smile of endless joy;
In ev'ry leaflet, every flower,
It traces an unfading bower,
   And bliss without alloy.

Love throws its halo on the forms
   And objects it designs;
And thus transfigured into grace,
Its ev'ry object, ev'ry place
   In Heavenly beauty shines.

This mortal dream of light and shade
   Will vanish with the night;
Life's wak'ning to reality
In peace and immortality
   And never waning light.

And sweet it is to rest assured
   That Truth shall victor be;
The shades of error all will blend
And haste their own destructive end,
   In dark mortality.

Their midnight but foretells the dawn
   Of Truth's eternal sun;
Their darkest hour will break the dream
And herald the awak'ning beam
   Of real life begun;—

The life with no vicissitudes,
   No alternating phase;
But harmony and music sweet—
Unfading light and joys complete—
   Unending love and praise.

Heavenward.

How shall we scatter and destroy the shades of earthly night?
When shall we see Love's plan revealed in God's eternal light?
When shall we hear the music roll unending, grand and sweet,
With no discordant note to mar its harmony complete?

Shall we, by drawing closer still the cerements of gloom,
Be rescued from the ills which would consign us to the tomb?
Ah, no! The pansy lifts its head to kiss the sunbeams bright,
And ev'ry little blade of grass springs up to greet the light.

As water doth its level seek, so must the Soul's desire,
E'en to its origin divine, unceasingly aspire.
"Let there be light!" and shades of ill will quickly pass away
Like dewdrops vanishing beneath the glorious orb of day.

The darkness that enshrouds the earth and hides the good from
    sight
Is but the shade of seeming ill—the absence of the light;
And all the shadows will disperse when Good reclaims its place,
We need but let the sunlight in and darkness flees apace.

Not outward scenes but inward joys make music in the Soul;
'Tis Heav'n brought nigh when Light and Love the heart and
    life control :
The state so beautiful and fair, of peace and light and love,
Is not a far-off, distant world, a fairy-land above :—

Not a locality remote—a place we know not where ;
Love needs no such prescribed abode to make its Eden fair ;
Love makes its Eden in the Soul that turns from death to life—
That into harmony translates Earth's discord and its strife.

Love makes the desert places bloom with roses of delight ;
It sheds its halo o'er the scene and banishes the night ;

It drowns all discord in the notes of harmony divine,
And makes Earth's lowliest abode in Heav'nly beauty shine.

Love makes fair Canaan's happy land, where milk and honey
   flow,
The Paradise where Palms of Life and flowers unfading grow :
It spreads the hungry Soul's repast with manna day by day :
Through pastures green, by waters still it kindly leads the way.

Love's mercies are not stored away in some far country blest,
To which our journey we must take ere we may feed and rest ;
We need but hunger, thirst and crave, and Love is at the door
Dispensing with its bounteous hand its all-sufficient store.

A full supply is ever near to meet the Soul's demand:
For ev'ry longing the response is waitingly at hand
To thirsty pilgrims faith reveals Love's Fountain brimming o'er
With waters of Eternal Life, refreshing evermore.

Beatitudes are not rewards attached to time or place,
They are the ever-present Good, the crowning joys of Grace :
And on these blest Beatitudes the hungry Soul may feed
In ev'ry state, in ev'ry place, in ev'ry hour of need.

We need not pass through death's dark vale ere Heaven can be
   won—
Its sweetness may be tested here, its pleasures now begun :
Hereby we know that we have passed from death e'en unto life,
When Love hath changed Earth's gloom to light, to concord all
   its strife.

"Let there light !" the echo comes reverberating still,
Until the music of the spheres doth Wisdom's plan fulfill :
And progress in the life divine will make our Heav'nward way
Grow brighter with each onward step unto "The Perfect Day."

FINIS.

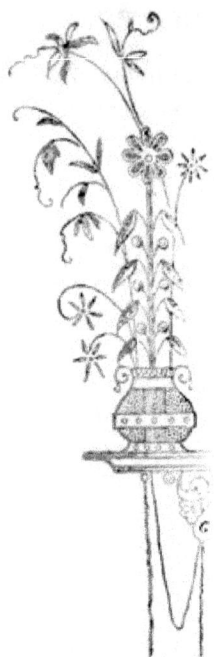

CONTENTS.

www.ingramcontent.com/pod-product-compliance
Lightning Source LLC
Chambersburg PA
CBHW021530270326
41930CB00008B/1171